Fervations
———————

Fervations

A poetic perspective of intimate love

Charles L. Hinsley

Linguistic Freedom Publications
Jamestown, NC

Copyright © 2015 Charles L. Hinsley

All rights reserved. No portion of this book may be reproduced mechanically, electronically, or by any other means, including photocopying, without written permission of the publisher. It is illegal to copy this book, post it to a website, or distribute it by any other means without permission from the publisher.

Published by Linguistic Freedom Publications
Jamestown, NC

Illustrations by Samuel Kwarteng
Back Cover Illustration: Ortis/Bigstock.com

ISBN 13: 978-0-9895873-2-7

Library of Congress Control Number: 2015900863

First Linguistic Freedom Publications printing: February 2015

Affirmation Page

These writings are dedicated to the
mysteries, complexities,
and
most compelling
emotion of human nature,
love!

For the intimations of the heart are not
constrained by the rigid rules
of our social human condition,
but rather, they respond to the power of nature's
divine law of attraction. Thus, the private
place of our inner soul must be
unafraid of the past and open to the possibilities
of uncertainty because love is mysterious
in that way . . .

And as life gradually enters into our soul awakening our spirit
each morning from its suspended state
of divine animation,
our intimate senses of passion and love
will release the sentiments
of our heart
because love is complex in that way . . .

*And the heart will ignore not the intimations of another
when the intimations of another heart
expresses true regard
because love is compelling in that way...*

*Every morning that we wake up we
have the opportunity to love!*

Table of Contents

The Prelude. 9

An Opening Tribute to Love 13

~ Chapter 1 ~
Validation of Love / 15

1. Fervations. 16
2. Ear Drops .20
3. Kisses in the Rain 22
4. Original Intentions. 24

~ Chapter 2 ~
Sentimental Feelings / 27

1. Inside My Soul 28
2. Illusionary Vision 31
3. Continuation of a Moment 33
4. Constant 35

~ Chapter 3 ~
Saying Hello and Then Good-bye / 39

1. Of Circumstance 40
2. A Solitary Confession 42
3. Secret Tears 45
4. A Long Time Ago Now 47

~ Chapter 4 ~
Love's Private Conversation with Intimacy / 49

1. The Essence of Love 50
2. Sensitivity 52
3. A. M. Company 54
4. The Unconditional Acceptance of a Beginning 56

~ Chapter 5 ~
Romantic Interludes / 59

1. A 21st Century Love Sonnet:
   Acapella Sentiments for My Beloved 60
2. Love Minuet #3:
   Ubiquitous Emotions of Sentimental Feelings 63
3. Intimate Persuasion 66
4. A Suitor's Mantra 68

A Closing Tribute to Love 73

The Prelude

It has been established through a divine decree that, "And now abideth faith, hope, love, these three; but the greatest of these is love." (1 Corinthians 13:13). This ordained positional truth establishes the proverbial foundation for which a man and a woman are to be committed to the sacred principle of honoring one another with complete unconditional regard. And it has also been decreed that God created male and female and blessed them to be fruitful and to multiple (Genesis 1:26–28).

The term that God has given this special and awesome gift of devotion and intimacy is called "agape` love". This is the highest level of human affection that God has commanded of mankind for which is to be shared between a man and a woman in the most intimate aspects of their relationship. Many times men and women find themselves struggling with the human conditions of loving one another without acknowledging the divine spiritual element that has been designed to nurture us through all of our relational shortcomings.

When the challenges of our interactions become clouded with doubt, mistrust, selfishness, and spite our relationship loses the strength to endure the long suffering that is a preeminent quality of agape` love. For without the committed desire and willingness of spirit to fight against the divisive onslaught of our misplaced arrogance and our conceited ego gratification, our relationships will suffer the consequences of broken heartedness. When this happens, we become harden and callous in our hearts to the idea that love can cure all things and we create an emotional barrier to prevent anyone from ever getting emotionally close to us again. We then consciously declare in our mind and we subconsciously internalize in our soul the negative affirmation that we will never let our emotions become vulnerable to that degree of hurt ever again. The pain of a broken heart penetrates deep into the soul.

However, if we can find the courage and the peace of mind to allow for the acceptance of God's word to penetrate the layers of insecurities and unforgiveness that we have created for ourselves, we will then be able to experience the over whelming healing power of agape` love. For the evidence of that power will be manifested through the giving of ourselves to His will so that His unconditional love for us as demonstrated through the sacrifice of His son's life on the cross will be revealed in our spiritual consciousness. And it will be at this point, that we will be able to recognize our dependency upon His omnipotent power and faithfully come to terms with the fact that we must reciprocate in kind with unconditional love for one another in order for us to experience the fruit of His gift which is agape` love.

This is a rare and seldom achieved level of intimacy; however, it is the level of intimacy that will sustain the long suffering of our commitment when the trials and tribulations of life attempt to defeat us. The special connectivity that two people will experience when the presence of divine wisdom abides within the quality of their love will be such that each person will be *able to fully comprehend the magnanimity of their togetherness and they will then be enlightened to the knowledge that their union is of a higher power greater than themselves. For they will also recognize that it is their responsibility to honor and respect their ordained status of divine intimacy with an equally committed devotion to one another.*

This is the premise for which the concept of "Fervations" has been birthed. Fervations is a state of being inspired by an intense passionate regard for a person of private adoration manifested from a spiritual dimension of unconditional love. When male meets female and the natural law of divine companionship rests and abides within their spirit of love, then the connectivity of their souls will join as one. And so, it is from this reflective insight into my own private experiences of having learned the subtle nuances of the male/female relationship for which I will now share with you a poetic perspective of intimate love.

An Opening Tribute to Love

*How might I explain the weight of your love
upon the frailty of my heart . . .
Prominent like the flowers that bloom in spring
from the refreshing rains of March.*

*Hindered by circumstances for which preclude
my love from being yours . . .
How might I explain the weight of your love
for which my heart affectionately adores.*

*As the sun rises each morning defiant against
the clutching grip of the wayward night . . .
Your love rises each day supplying my heart with
a new breath of life.*

*Your love seems immense while standing on the
shores of uncertain feelings . . .
Unable to cross the raging seas of emotional turbulence
my heart wanders endlessly.*

*I walk in the shadow of your humble love with your
silhouette the focus of my affections . . .
My heart is prepared to stand full guard and provide
your love life-long protection.*

*How might I explain the weight of your love
upon the frailty of my heart . . .
Daunting in its immensity for it overshadows
my love like a cloud of dark.*

*Your love is incomparable to other loves
I have once known . . .
The majestic reverence of your unheralded divineness
makes your love stand alone.*

*Restrained from the sensual pleasure of enjoying the
tender comfort of your embrace . . .
I compensate my loneliness by praying for the
strengthening of my faith.*

*How might I explain the weight of your love
upon the frailty of my heart . . .
To wit thus I offer my plea that my love
will never ever part!*

~ Until the end of time my love will be endless ~

Chapter 1

Validation of Love

"Listen to Your Heart"

Fervations

*We spoke to each other in silence . . . listening to the
quietness of sound's whispering echoes of love and
only our hearts could interpret the words.*

*I spoke to her directly from the gender
of my masculine creation
and she responded to me equally from the nature
of her femininity.*

. . . Words of love spoken without saying a word . . .

*Our hearts listened closely to the words of our emotions
as they spoke intensely about the intimacy of our love . . .
a commitment so deep that the reverberations of our passion
produced an indelible feeling
of sensual bliss that could only be felt
by two people joined as one.*

*I spoke to her as I wished for her to speak to me
saying those things which could not be said with words
and could not be understood with just our minds . . .
but understood only when spoken intensely
from the sensibilities of our hearts.*

*Words transcending the boundaries of the decibels of sound
and expressing the exhilarating power*

*of our feelings as they permeated the barrier between
male and female; man and woman; companions and lovers.*

*As we talked to one another in the language of love
our conversation conveyed the sincerity
of our unconditional trust,
. . . here again was
a moment where words were spoken without saying a word.*

*We were engaged in the art of unspoken communication
when my soul connected with her soul
and we became soul mates
for all eternity . . .
Sharing our past, discussing our present,
and planning our future,
all in the context of knowing that our ability to speak
with our hearts depended upon
learning the vocabulary of the unspoken language of love.*

*How profound it is to know of another when two people
can speak without uttering a word . . .
for the power of true love has no voice,
it simply expresses itself in unconditional terms.
A condition of reciprocated dialogue
between uninhibited emotions
stimulated by a connectedness between two intimate souls
and causing both hearts to understand the
spiritual dimension of their total love.
The awesome beauty of love's non-verbal expression can*

*only be experienced when two hearts
are linked together in a deep
abiding faith
and the faith proclaimed must be proclaimed intensely from
the sensibilities of one's heart
and then you will come to know the true essence
of
fervations . . .
an indescribable feeling of divine love!*

~ from a perspective of intimate love ~

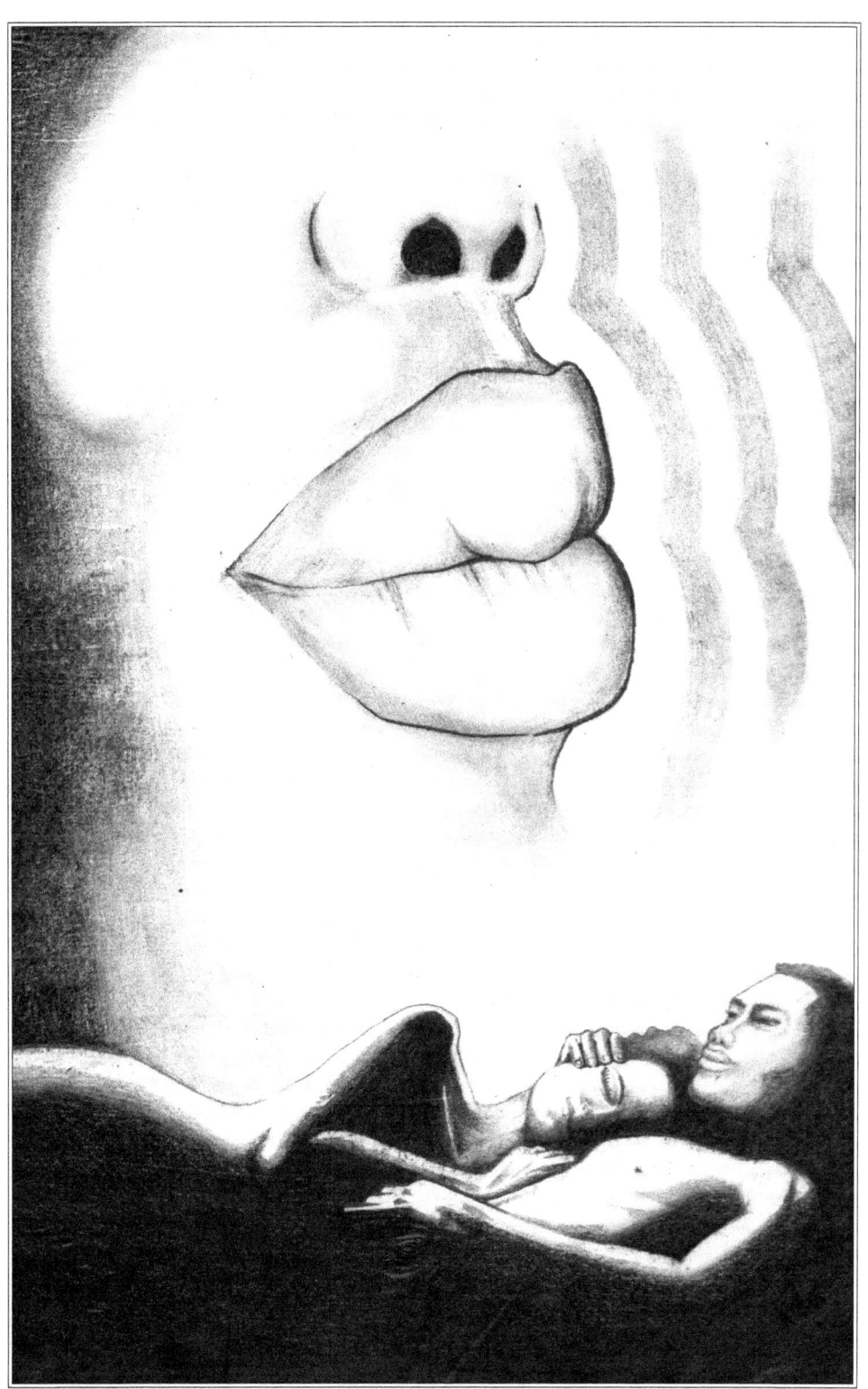

Ear Drops

*I whispered in her ear . . . "I love you"
and the medicinal effect
of my words
medicated her soul and soothed the discomfort
of
her heart.*

~ love cures all manner of pain ~

Kisses in the Rain

*The clouds of the heavens began to cry
and the emotions of their sorrow poured
down upon my face . . .
but, I was not alone for she was standing there too.*

*Hand-in-hand we stood paralyzed gazing
into each other's eyes . . . tear drops from
the heavens above blended
with the tear drops of her own . . .*

*My purpose was to stop the tears from falling,
so I kissed
her
in the rain.*

~ love is sufficient unto love ~

Kahlil Gibran

Original Intentions

In an effort to express an original soliloquy for the indescribable sentiments of my emotions that lay dormant within the vestibule of my soul and are secretly yearning for their moment of opportunity to reveal the truth of their intense adoration for you I must dwell deep into the reservoir of the inner sanctum of my heart to earnestly try and bring forth a persuasive understanding so that it will allow me to make sense to you my romantic intentions such that when I attempt to articulate the profound joy of my unconditional love for you that the relevant truth of its meaning will be intrinsically felt through an unspoken connectivity that will make it seem all so simple but yet, make it unequivocally clear that my tenderness for you is genuine, purposeful, and singular in its intent to make the existence of your being comforted with every utterance of affection that proceedth out of my mouth directed toward you and by doing so create a sense within your soul of a unique specialness never before experienced and henceforth never again to be duplicated because the concept of my love for you is predicated upon an emotional intrinsic truth that declares as its premise the concept that if I engage in the proverbial act of extending my love to you with all my heart and soul and I respectfully introduce to you extraordinary feelings of divinely inspired affinity, you my love will become emotionally inclined to reciprocate with mutual affections and thus, it will then become prudent of me to test the theory of loving you to see if my personal love plus your personal love will equal our eternal love together and thereby prove the undeniable effects of our emotional intrinsic connection concluding with the outcome being you plus me equaling our love enjoined eternally and it will be through this manner of proclivity that my desired notions of exposing my laden feelings to you will be communicated in provocative terms of endearment to make my presence in your life true and permanent but most significantly, authentic and original.

~ evidence of an original love ~

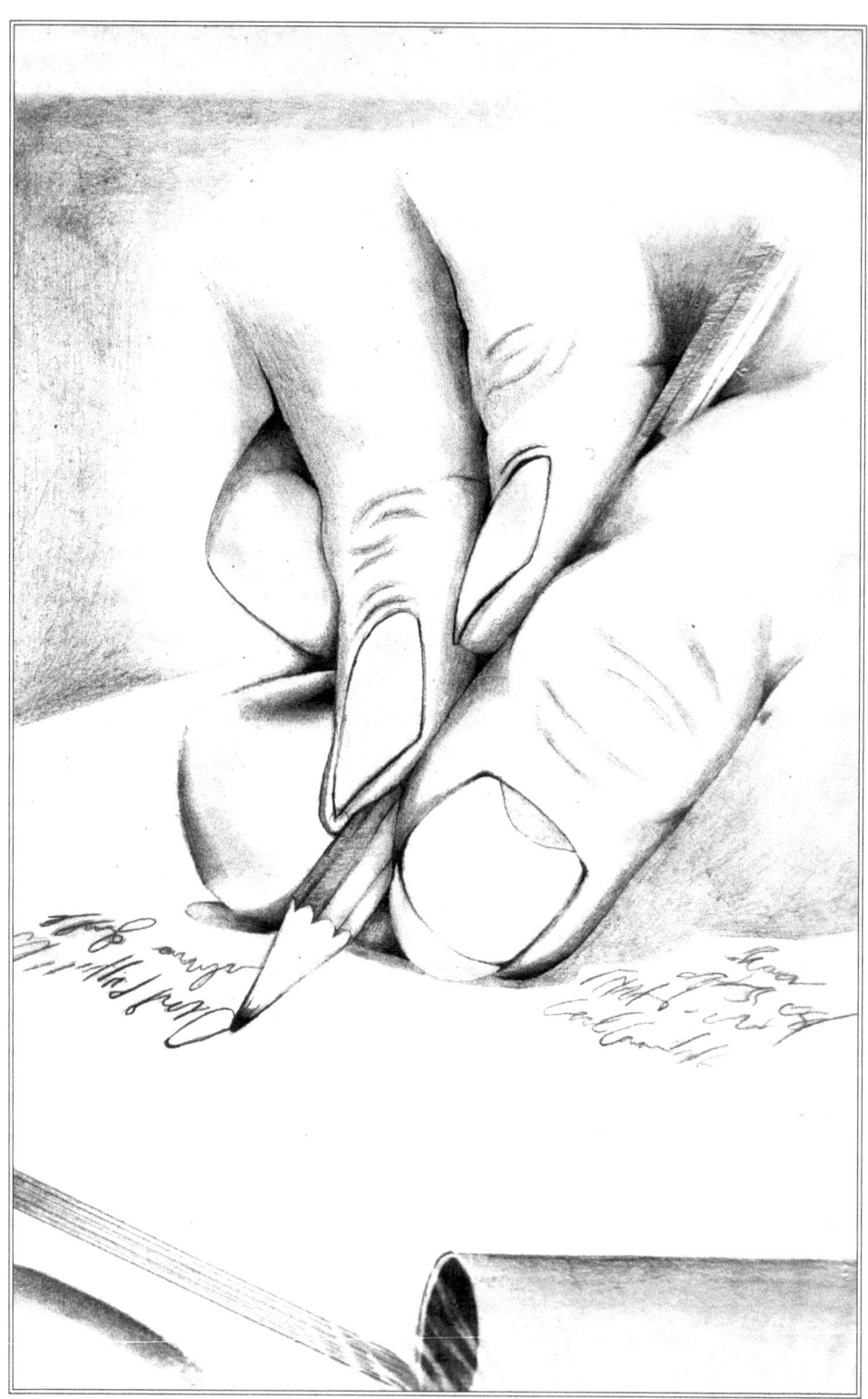

Chapter 2

Sentimental Feelings

*"Only love affects the sensibilities
of the heart that makes
joy and pain inseparable"*

Inside My Soul

Inside the mind of my soul I think about the privacy
of your foreign nature . . . Why, I ask
do you intrigue me so, I search my heart deeply hoping
that it will know.

Inside the mind of my soul I think about the essence
of your total being . . . Why, I ask
does the presence of your absence make me feel lonely inside
I will forgo all
my pride just to be close to you.

Inside the mind of my soul I think about the passion
of your intimate embrace . . . Why, I ask
does the memory of your scent make me shiver, I wish
that I could deliver the answer to the
mystery of your world.

Inside the mind of my soul I think about the sensual
temperament of your affectionate nature . . . Why,
I ask does the sensitivity of your intuition excite the nature
of my masculinity and cause such intense virility
that I yearn for the day of your complete exclusivity.

Inside the mind of my soul I think about the gift
you have become in my life . . . Why, I ask
does the depth of your trust seem like no other, I hope not

to smother the joy you offer . . . so I pray not
to be afraid if our friendship turns
into lovers.

———————————

~ inside the mind of my soul I think about her ~

Illusionary Vision

The silhouette of a long ago memory repeatedly came in and
out of focus,
taunting the recall of my mind about whether
my love was real or not.
I tried to perceive the image of its outline through
the foggy haze of my doubt . . . trying to trace days unknown.
What manner of illusion had this
shadow of a doubt cast against the wall of my reality?
Surely the sensibilities of my heart would provide
me the answer. But the image seemed
to portray itself as a mysterious enigma with the perception
of it truth hidden by layers of uncertain emotions.

(the obscurity of feelings oftentimes distort the truth)

And I was still left searching through the
mist of its vagueness when it suddenly became evident that
time had reduced the visibility of my memory.
What was I to do? How was I to learn of its
meaningfulness to me if this image continued to repeatedly
make itself unknown.
Obviously, the passionate intensity of my heart would
have to evaporate the misty vapor
that blurred my vision so
the meaning of its elusive past would become clear.

~ your heart will always remember true love
even when your mind cannot ~

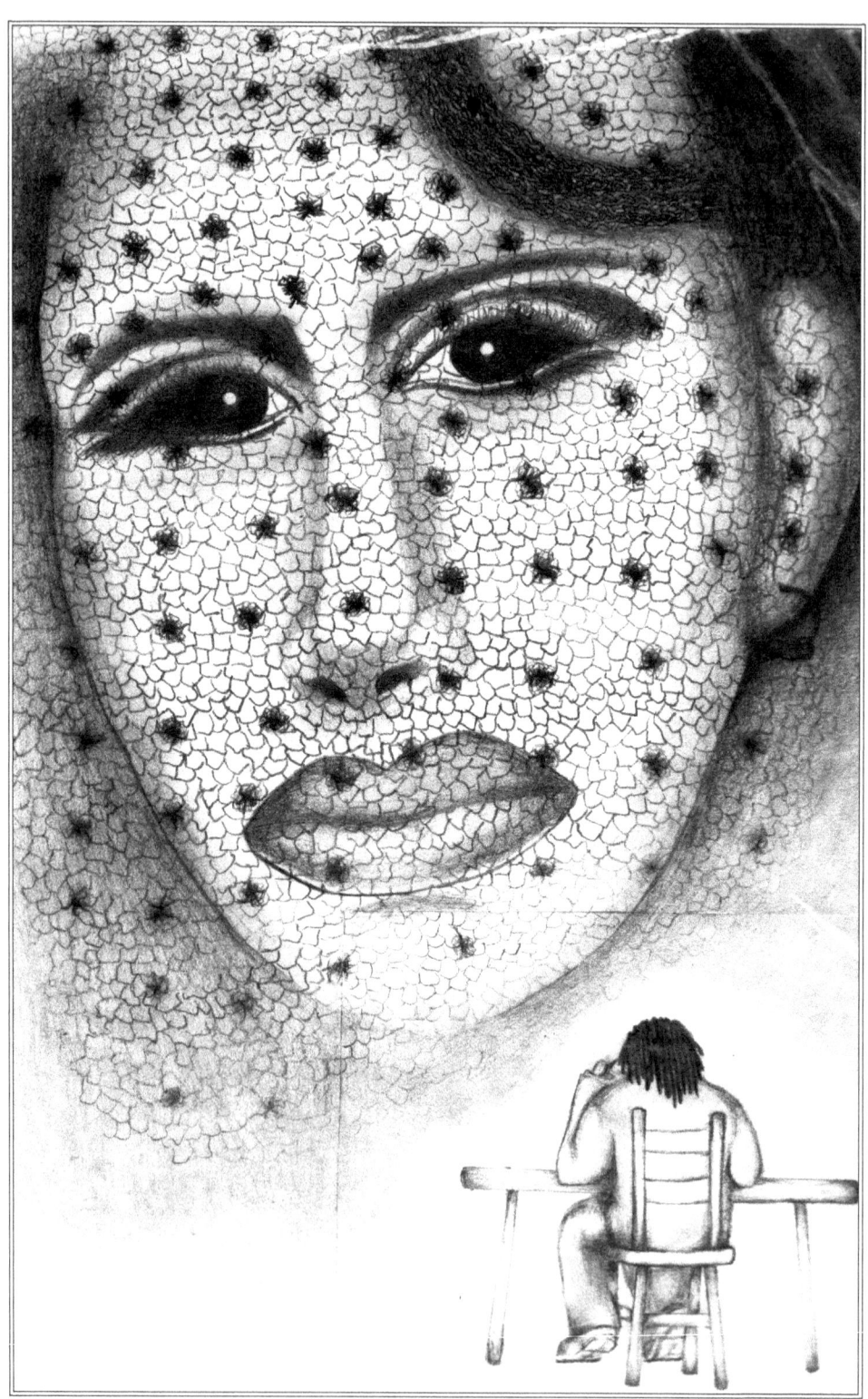

Continuation of a Moment

... and when the morning after had come
and the dawn of a new day quietly
peeped through the window,
our love was renewed from the night before.
She, my leading lady, and I, her leading man
rehearsing our love scene
for the romantic love story of our lives.
Entwined in hopes, entangled in commitment,
and linked together by faith, the nakedness of our
vulnerable emotions laid motionless and exposed
as our bodies touched ever so gently.
Caressing each other closely and not allowing
the smallest part of our flesh to be untouched
we concentrated on loving
one another as deeply as our love would allow.
Our words to each other were spoken
in whispers mimicking the
softness of the moment, but our reply
was heard in the grand canyon of our
hearts and vibrated with
thunderous echoes of exuberating intensity.
Innocent in its beginning, serious in its in between,
and incredibly life changing in the end ...
and the continuation of our moment would repeat itself
again, and again, and again ...

~ the compatibility of intimate love is extraordinary ~

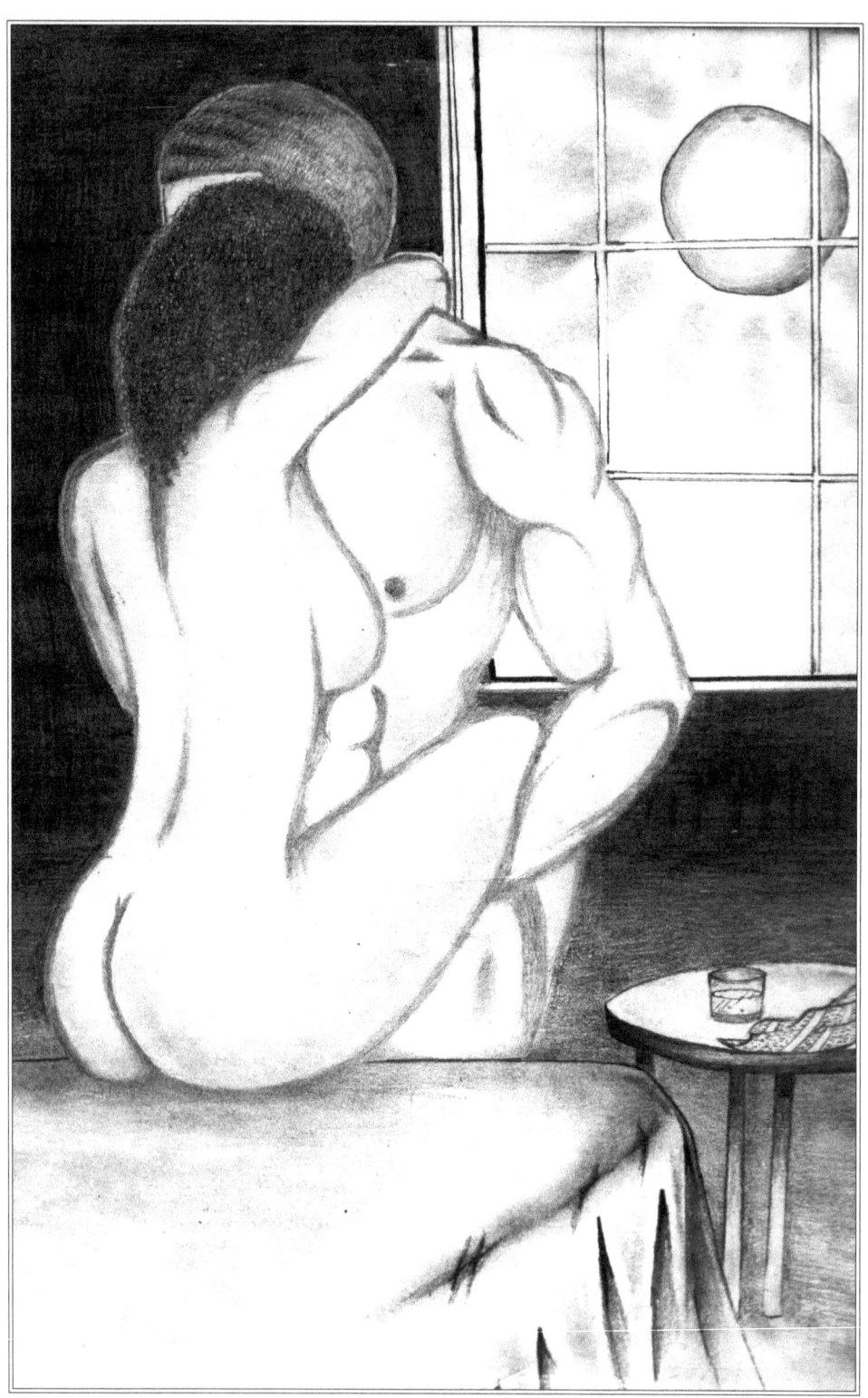

Constant

*In the inner core of my being you are there . . .
pulsatingly, intensely, exuberatingly reminding me why I care*

*Like a memory of a once-upon-a-time love affair
. . . reoccurring over and over and over again . . .
Sensing feelings of passionate intimacies that I wish to share,
constantly reminding me of a love that will never end*

*In the inner core of my being you are there . . .
unrelenting, unwavering, penetrating like a piercing stare*

*Like the churning current of a rushing waterfall
. . . pounding fiercely against the rocks below . . .
The emotions of my heart trembles at the sound of your call,
and the depth of my passion I want you to know*

*In the inner core of my being you are there . . .
tugging, nudging, throbbing incessantly in my heart's lair*

*Like the descending power of a cascading avalanche
. . . rushing downward by the force of gravity's might . . .
My private desires respond naturally to
our emotional circumstance,
they react uncontrollably all day and all night*

In the inner core of my being you are there . . .
pondering, speculating, reminiscing
continuously for me to remain aware

Like the exuberant expression displayed
when two lovers reunite
. . . the exhilaration they share is waiting to explode . . .
As the poet within me try to find the right words to recite,
you are ever present, everywhere, and all through my soul . . .
constant!

~ you are there ~

Chapter 3

Saying Hello and Then Good-bye

*"Love will make you sigh,
love will make you cry,
love will make you say good-bye,
but true love will never die!"*

Of Circumstance

*We came together by circumstances of which we were not
certain of the meaning, but knowing only
that we were unashamed of who we were. We accepted each
other without protest; her for her and me for me.
Although different in our nature and different in our past,
we were the same in our need; a need to feel
appreciated, a need to feel loved, a need to have a friend
in an unknown place;
and there we stood on common ground.
And through our commonality we shared our needs
and became friends in an unknown place;
united in friendship with a
new-found hope, we discovered a new-found love,
a love we never knew could exist.
And yet, as time moved on we could no longer accept
each other for who we were . . .
I, a man with faults in need of a deeper understanding
and she, a woman with faults
in need of a deeper compassion. And she felt betrayed by the
the frailty of my human condition and I too,
felt betrayed by her lack of faith in love's power
to restore all things . . .
and so, we again stood alone,
but this time on uncommon ground
and still unashamed of who we were.*

~ we live and we learn ~

A Solitary Confession

In my moment of solitude
My intentions are not to be rude
But here and now will I express
The love I truly wish to confess
Oh, how triumphant you made me feel
To have caught a love so ideal
The love you gave I did not expect
Your tender love I could not reject
So sweet and innocent you would act
You captured my heart and that's a fact
Always giving, never would you take
And you only gave for love's sake
Polite and charming in every respect
You rewarded my heart with joy to collect
So unselfish with your love
You, I would always dream of
A finer love I never knew
And each day my affection grew
Underneath my flesh beat a heart so sincere
I long to be forever near
Life with you was oh so grand
Our togetherness seemed like the perfect plan
Enchanted by your girlish smile
And captivated by your feminine style
You imprisoned my love by nature's law
And natural love is never a flaw

But now your love is only a perception
The mirror of my mind is its only reflection
Your tender love my mind won't elude
For it comforts me in my deepest solitude.

~ Solitude is the stillness of your soul that seeks the truth ~

Secret Tears

*I cried last night,
the only witness was my heart . . .
tears frozen behind the serenity of my eyes
dark brown disguise.*

*I hurt some
but tears never come
cause a man ain't suppose to cry.*

~ sitting on the dock of the bay ~

A Long Time Ago Now

Several sunsets had already eclipsed the time zone
of my loneliness . . . for I yearned deeply
for the presence of her being. The shadow of her absence was
reminiscent of a once-upon-a-time love affair
that ended with a goodbye.
And I was afraid, afraid that déjà vu would become reality
all over again.
It was a long time ago now that I was in love with her
and she in love with me . . .
but this time was of different reasons for why our
souls could not be together. the
understanding of why I felt this way was completely foreign
to me . . . I just simply knew that I missed her
and yet, it resembled a moment in my
life a long time ago now . . .
I wondered what it all
meant?

~ she once said goodbye a long time ago ~

Chapter 4

Love's Private Conversation with Intimacy

*"When the gentle tenderness of love's
soft spoken affections
are whispered into our ears,
the effectual virtue of love's power
penetrates all levels of hurt
and comforts our deepest
and inner most desires
to be loved"*

The Essence of Love

*On pondering this matter on many occasions
there seems to be a noticeable fundamental relation.
Take for instance the tenderness of a
touch combined with the brightness of a smile,
implying that you mean so much and
your affection is worthwhile.
The joy you receive from the sound of laughter stimulated
by the gayness of your play while anxiously
waiting for the after, making love when the sun fades away.
Sharing secrets that only the two of you
will ever know and planning the life you want to live,
while each day your love tends to grow
and each giving all you can give.
Calling one another perhaps two and three times a day
saying how much you've been missed;
daydreaming about the other
when you're away and thinking about that soft sweet kiss.
You share many ups and downs and sometimes
may have feelings of regret, but you are
able to forgive each frown
because you've not only learned to love
but also to respect.*

~ love is as love does ~

Sensitivity

Words are not always the best

way to say

what one has to say . . .

so I sometimes speak

without saying a

word.

. . . s s s h!

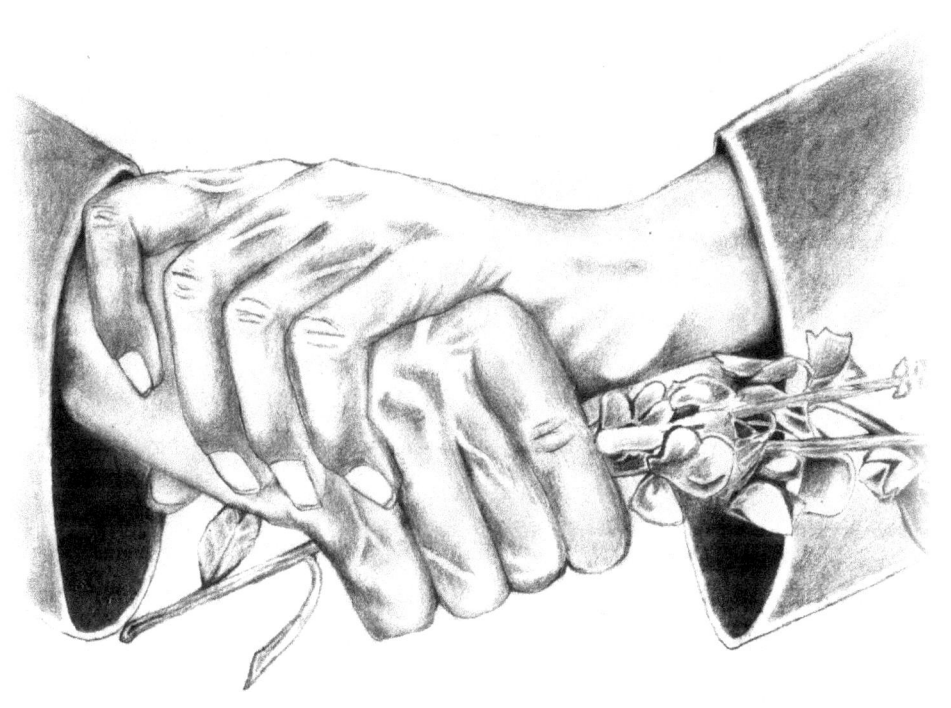

A. M. Company

*Committed to the feelings
that bonded us together . . .
Connected by the trust
that we held for one another . . .
Conformed by the spiritual
power of agape` love . . .
the passionate intensity of our early morning intimacy
confirmed that we were
made for each
other
at
2:47 a.m.*

~ human nature ~

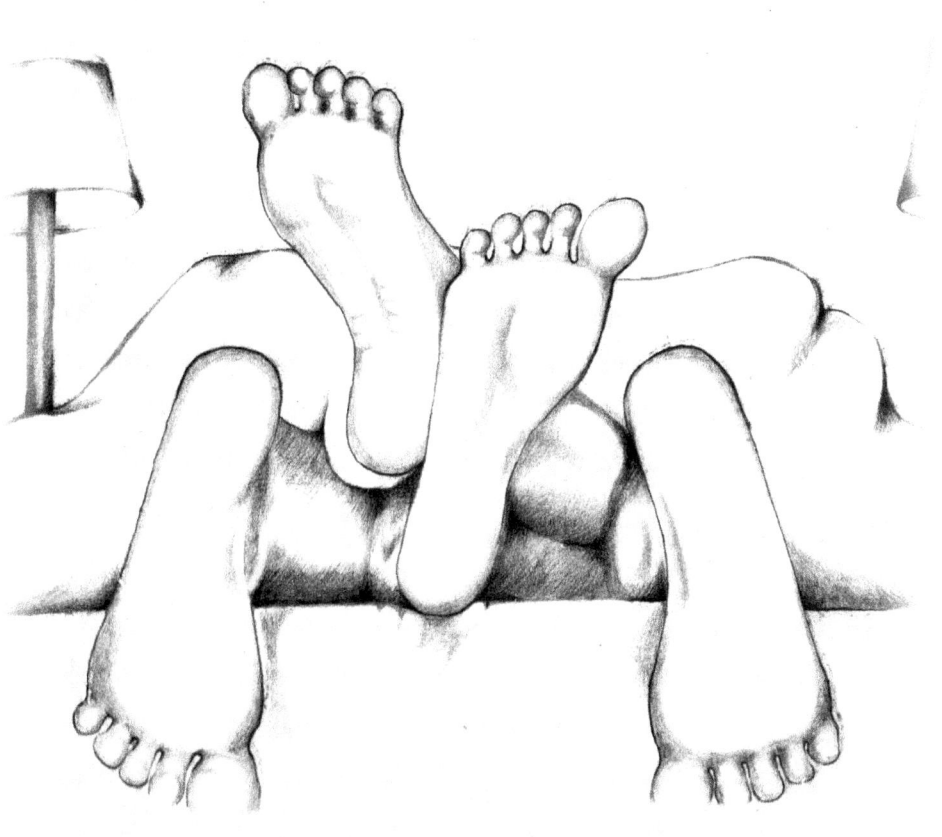

The Unconditional Acceptance of a Beginning

Amidst the depth of my contemplation I could sense the heaviness of her consternation about the troublesomeness of my worry although my thoughts did not scurry to arrive at a conclusion that was not an illusion of my imagination so I tried another approach in hopes that I could relieve her concerns while trying to help her learn how deep my feelings had become and all the while she studied my style and offered back her sweet tender smile to communicate to me that it was okay with her for me to expose the residue of my past without her judgment being cast and also for me to know that life is not so that I could ever predict its future much less understand all its confusion because the sensibilities of the heart brings forth light to the dark and joy comes from the simplicity of sharing another's love when sprinkled with blessings from above but only then did it make sense to me that the pretense of my efforts would wane helplessly against the strength of her sensitive compassion and instantly I realized that I had to surrender to the subtle romance of her charm while drifting into the pleasing comfort of her arms and sentimentally sealing my fate with a kiss which I would be remised not to say how the softness of her lips blew me away like the freshness of the Southern rains that came from out of nowhere and blended with the tears of my inner pain because of the notion that she would never be mine in the short span of my lifetime but the gleam in her eyes made me realize that our moment must be cherished for that which it is and the beauty of that moment would last us past the forever times of our years if only she would allow the unconditional acceptance of our beginning to be the key that unlocks the door to the precious gift of our eternal memories.

~ I wanted to expose all my love to her ~

Chapter 5

Romantic Interludes

"Chivalry and honor are the inherent
qualities of love that
makes the innocence of a courtship
blossom into
a
genuine romance"

A 21ˢᵗ Century Love Sonnet: Acapella Sentiments for My Beloved

I bequeath to thee my love for thee until the setting
 of eternity...
I love thee for love only in my lifetime of summer
 delight;
The flower petals of thy eyes evoke the interest of my
 sight.
Tis the cool breath of thy gentle summer breeze that
 caresses my face;
Wind gusts from mountain top peaks whisper of thy
 heavenly grace.
From whence thy beauty comes the color of rainbow
 shades;
Intricate patterns of garden flowers to wit thy beauty
 is made.

Delicate as the morning dew from whence thy love shows
 its innocence;
The acapella sentiments of a lovebird's song inspire
 heaven's contentment.
Oh lady of mine from whence thy love abounds within my
 soul;
Thy majestic elegance was gifted to thee and thy love
 was made manifold.

*To wit, thus I dare to speak forbidden words shackled
    to my tongue;
Words attempting to break their bondage to scream out
    my beloved!
I bequeath to thee my love for thee until the setting
    of eternity...*

*My lady Marie, my lady Marie, wherefore art thou is my
    lady Marie!*

~ A contemporary Shakespearean love poem ~

Love Minuet #3: Ubiquitous Emotions of Sentimental Feelings

Inspiration has given courage to the
shyness of my thoughts . . .
allowing my love to escape from the dungeon of my heart.

My love for thee rises with the stellar
light of the early morning sun . . .
My love is awakened and thus given life
from whence thy purpose comes.
Ancient whispers of antiquity to wit
thy love speaks her claim,
Tell of ubiquitous emotions of sentimental
feelings that speaketh of a love unashamed.
Thy love is as fresh as a cool meadow brook
boarded by yellow daffodil faces,
It whispers secrets of a romantic love from
the ancient past of lullaby places.

I wish of intimate longings with thee to be among
the falling stars of the moonlit sky . . .
Dancing across heaven's way displaying
my love flame for you and I.
Eternity has the key to infinity and thus it
holds the secret to our predestined plan,

*My love for thee is waiting for thee in
the palm of our Master's hand.
The loveliness of thee abounds from the
beauty of life that boldly comes forth,
Your majestic reverence is like the eternal light
of the guiding night star of the North.*

*From season to season thy love for thee
will always remain the same . . .
The winter snowdrifts of my heart melt away
with the coming of love's springtime rains.
I speak not bashfully of my renowned devotion of thee,
For my heart knoweth of the joy you bring
and the love you have set free.
The shimmering glare of the moonlight's glow
that reflects off the surface of a pond . . .
Is a reflection of my faithful love for thee that
will last for all eternity and beyond!*

*Inspiration has given courage to the
shyness of my thoughts . . .
allowing my love to escape from the dungeon of my heart.*

~ a love inspired by love ~

Intimate Persuasion

*Wrapped in a moment of private seclusion and
isolated from the distractions of the
world's intrusions. Preparing to discover the sensual nature
of each other and anticipating the pleasure of
becoming intimate lovers.*

*Engulfed by the mystic of sharing a cherished moment of
time, the sensual ambience of our romance was
complimented with wine.
Romantically celebrating this most special
of occasions, our human natures
responded naturally to this intimate persuasion.*

. . . and then, we made love!

~ the secret of true intimacy is romance ~

A Suitor's Mantra

Oh thy lady of my heart
Wherefore art thou shall I start
My heart knoweth of no passion so true
Thy fragrant scent, thy color blue
Our destiny was not of mere blind fate
Heaven created us to be soul mates
The depth of thy beauty is undisputed
To honor thy charm is my solemn duty
Heaven sent down a divine angel
My heart chose to secretly claim her
As light brings forth joy to the dark
Thy presence flatters the emotions of my heart
Words and whispers of gentle affections
Speaketh of thy longing for intimate connections

Oh thy lady of my heart
Wherefore art thou shall I start
In the midst of eternity's chosen fate
The desires of my heart will patiently wait
To thee my love is purposely sent
Know that I long to sit upon your heart bench
In time thy emotions will surely know
Whence come the power of the moonlight's glow
Enchanted with the glow of a full crested moon
Lullabies of love songs will make thy heart swoon
Private emotions I must confess

Thy sentiments of passion fill my chest
I walk amongst thy garden rose
Thy fragrant scent tickles my nose

Oh thy lady of my heart
Wherefore art thou shall I start
Divine in nature thy soul content
Divine in love from heaven sent
Incandescent eyes reveal thy strength
The beauty of thy soul my heart can sense
Two hearts joined by the power of trust
Respect and honor this I must
Thy love I behold in high esteem
Melodies of joy doeth my heart does sing
Oh friend of mine whence I so claim
Thy offer of my love I won't be ashamed
A suitor's plea hence this I speak
Thy precious love my heart thus seek

Oh thy lady of my heart
Wherefore art thou shall I start
Rainbow colors paint the sky
'Tis the sign of heaven's blessings for you and I
Fairy tale dreams of love and romance
Compatible hearts is our fate of circumstance
Inspired by the notion of a love so true
Each day I seek the celebration of you
Amongst the grandeur of all the earth
Nothing compares with thy precious worth
From thy heart thus thee I pledge

My life commitment thus this I said
Thy passionate soul is full of youth
Your eternal love is my visionary truth

Oh thy lady of my heart
Wherefore art thou shall I start

———————————

~ from the pages of a suitor's heart ~

A Closing Tribute to Love

*Because of you, my world has forever
changed and the simplicity of my
life will never ever be the same. The way in which
I now view the world is not like I once
did . . . I view it now with true love
resonating deep within my heart and not with the
infatuation of a childish kid.
The stars at night have a different
meaning to me now . . . I have purpose
in my soul when I once use to
wonder how? How could I be so alone amongst the
camaraderie of life's wondrous pleasures . . . I didn't
have you in my life is my heart's rhetorical answer.
The sound of silence has its own distinctive sound,
and listening to the sentiments of your love
has made my life more profound.*

*I now know of the real joy of an innocent moment of shared
laughter because you helped me understand
through our intimate pleasures of
the morning after.
Life use to seem so unreal to all my emotional senses,
but because of you, the reality of love's divine
purpose has penetrated all my defenses.*

*I never had the courage to shout out loud
for love from the top of my voice,
but now that I have discovered your
love, I shout without remorse!
Not a day goes by without me having
a renewed sense of life . . .
the freshness of the early morning dew reminds me that
loving you is just right.*

*In the midst of my insecurities when I
questioned why had love eluded me,
you came along and gave meaning to my life's true destiny.
My destiny was revealed through a divinely inspired truth . . .
the presence of your existence has given my life meaning
and my love is all because
of
you!*

www.ingramcontent.com/pod-product-compliance
Lightning Source LLC
Chambersburg PA
CBHW050606300426
44112CB00013B/2100